MORE CREATIVE CRAFTS for KIDS

Reader's Digest
Children's Books®

Pleasantville, New York • Montréal, Québec • Bath, United Kingdom

Parent Letter

More Creative Crafts for Kids is a child's passport to many fun and unique crafts. In each themed section, children will discover a wide variety of crafts as well as interesting facts and helpful tips that accompany the projects.

Each craft contains a list of materials needed for each project. Parents should help gather all the materials before beginning each craft. For safety or convenience, consider substituting materials when possible. Some crafts should be done with adult supervision, which are indicated by this symbol, ✔.

Remember, children should be encouraged to explore their own imaginations and not be restricted by any suggested designs or colors. There is so much to discover in **More Creative Crafts for Kids** —enjoy!

Edited by Alicia Zadrozny
Designed by Mabel Zorzano
All crafts originally conceived by Martine Cesar
Translated from the original French by Donna Vekteris

Published by Reader's Digest Children's Books, Reader's Digest Road, Pleasantville, NY U.S.A. 10570-7000 and Reader's Digest Children's Publishing Limited, The Ice House, 124-126 Walcot Street, Bath UK BA1 5BG
© 2008, 2006 Martine Cesar, Artkids Company.
All rights reserved. Reader's Digest Children's Books, the Pegasus logo, and Reader's Digest are all registered trademarks of The Reader's Digest Association, Inc.
Manufactured in China.
10 9 8 7 6 5 4 3 2 1

CONTENTS

ANIMAL CRAFTS

Animal Boxes

MATERIALS

- Cardboard box (from a computer or sound system, for example)
- Strong glue
- Pencil
- Black marker
- Acrylic paints
- Paintbrushes
- Foam paint roller
- Scissors
- Box cutter or art knife

1

On cardboard, draw a round shape for the duck's head, a triangle for its tail, and a long, narrow oval for its beak.

2

Cut out the pieces. Fold the beak twice, leaving a 1-inch band in the middle.

HINT
If you'd like, you can follow the same basic steps to make the lion shown here.

3

Glue the head and tail to the box. Glue the middle band of the beak to the head that's already been glued to the box.

4

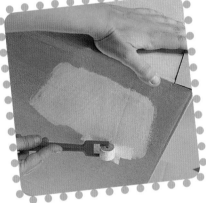

Paint the duck white. Allow it to dry.

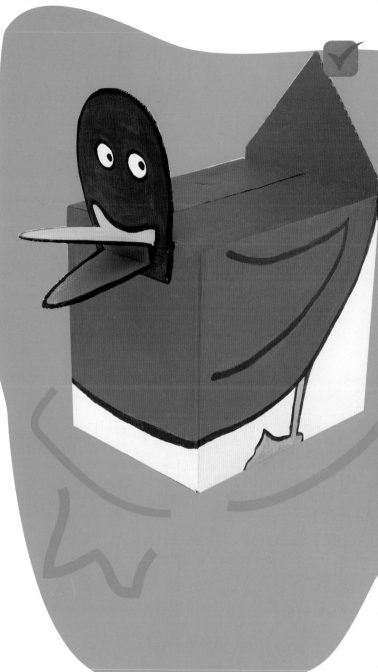

5

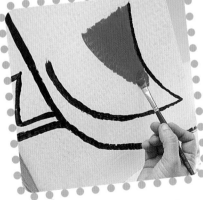

Paint the outline of the duck, the wings and the feet black.

6

Paint the rest of the duck red, yellow, white and black as shown.

MATERIALS

Giraffe and Ladybug

- Styrofoam balls in different sizes
- Wooden skewers
- Yellow, red, black and white construction paper
- Acrylic paint and paintbrushes
- Glue
- Scissors and art knife
- Pipe cleaners

Spotted red or spotted black, these two cute characters are easy to make out of Styrofoam balls and construction paper. Just follow the instructions carefully.

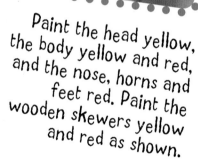

1

Cut two medium Styrofoam balls in two for the feet.

2

Paint the head yellow, the body yellow and red, and the nose, horns and feet red. Paint the wooden skewers yellow and red as shown.

3

Glue on the nose and eyes. Paint the pupils black. Use short bits of skewer for the horns and tail. Stick two small red balls onto the horns.

4

Glue bits of pipe cleaner to the tail and head. Cut ears out of yellow construction paper. Cut two slits in the head and insert the ears.

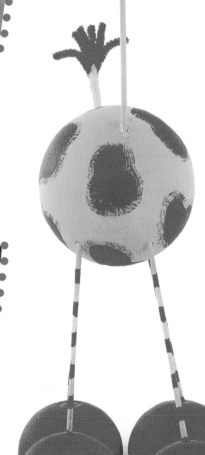

1 Draw an oval on red construction paper for the body. Cut it out.

2 Cut half an oval out of black construction paper for the head. Glue it on to the body.

3 Cut four slits in the body as shown. Fold them inward so they overlap slightly and tape them together.

4 Cut the eyes, nose, antennae, legs and spots out of colored construction paper as shown. Glue them on.

5 Stick a wooden skewer through a small Styrofoam ball and pass it through the sides of the ladybug to make it roll!

Paper Whale

Made of paper and cardboard, this whale rides over the waves and is ready to perch in a flowerpot or any other solid base.

Draw the whale on the cardboard and cut it out.

Tear strips of newspaper or magazine and glue them onto the whale.

MATERIALS

- Corrugated cardboard
- Magazines or newspapers
- Glue
- Paintbrushes
- Blue and white poster paint
- Scissors
- Wooden Skewer
- Empty tissue box
- Sand

3

Let it dry well. Give it an undercoat of white paint, and then paint blue over it.

4

Paint the facial tissue box blue, let dry, and then paint a wave on it. Fill the box with sand.

5

Paint the skewer blue or white. Insert one end into the base of the whale.

6

Stand the whale in the box. You can make a zebra, too, following the same basic directions.

Animal Frames

With some cardboard, pipe cleaners, and a few beads you can make these funny picture holders.

MATERIALS

- Corrugated cardboard
- Acrylic paint and paintbrushes
- Scissors and art knife
- Pipe cleaners
- Glue
- Wood or plastic beads

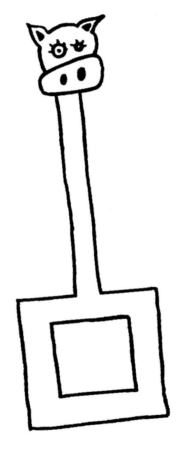

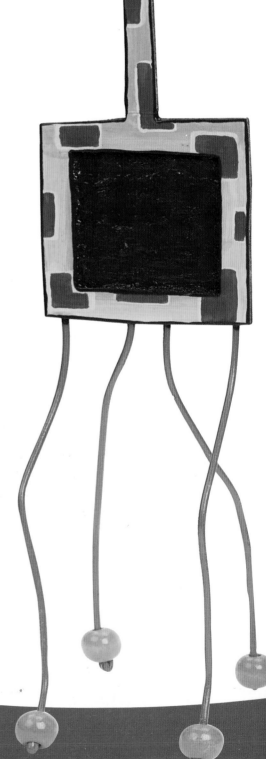

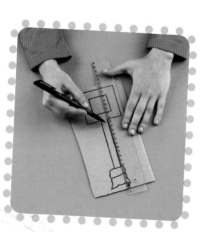

1

Draw the giraffe with its frame as shown. Cut out the giraffe as well as a square in the middle.

2

Paint the giraffe. Let it dry. Cut a square from the cardboard the same size as the giraffe's body. Paint it black. When it's dry, glue it to the back of frame.

3

Insert pipe cleaners into the head and the bottom of the frame. Attach beads to the ends of the pipe cleaners and glue them in place.

Bubble Wrap Crocodile

This crocodile is easy to make out of a sheet of bubble wrap and some cardboard.

1

Roll the bubble wrap into a tube that is narrow at one end. This is your crocodile's body. Slip a 5-inch piece of wire into the narrow end, which is the tail. Tape the bubble wrap underneath the crocodile so it doesn't unroll. Bend the tail.

Paint the body with green acrylic paint, and then add a few touches of yellow. Let it dry.

2

MATERIALS

- Sheet of bubble wrap
- Corrugated cardboard
- Red cardboard
- Pencil
- Acrylic paint
- Scissors and art knife
- Multi-purpose glue
- Double-sided tape
- Metal wire
- Styrofoam balls

3 Cut four feet out of corrugated cardboard and paint them green. Cut the crest out of red cardboard. Cut a slit in the back of the crocodile.

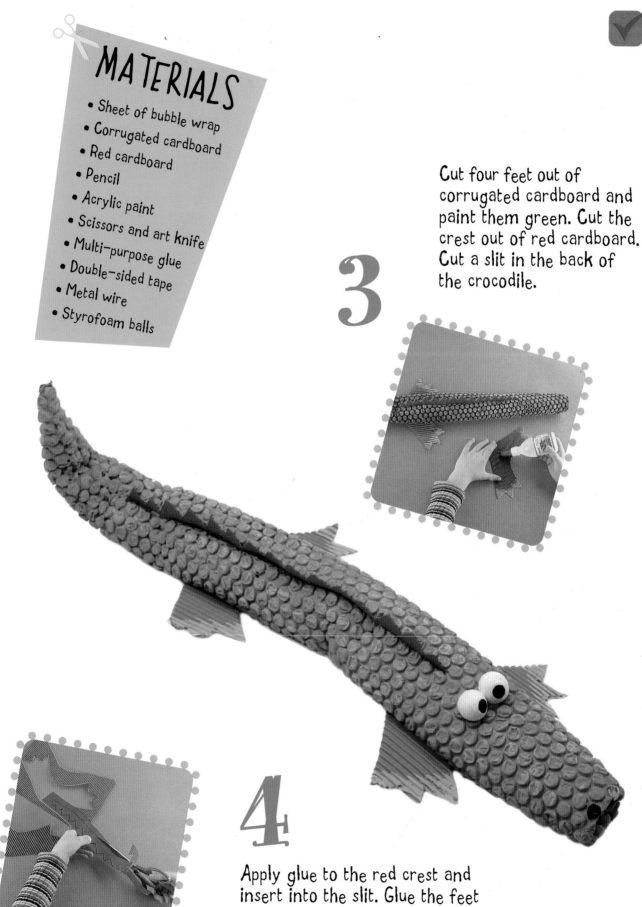

4 Apply glue to the red crest and insert into the slit. Glue the feet to the bottom of the crocodile. Glue on the eyes and paint the pupils black.

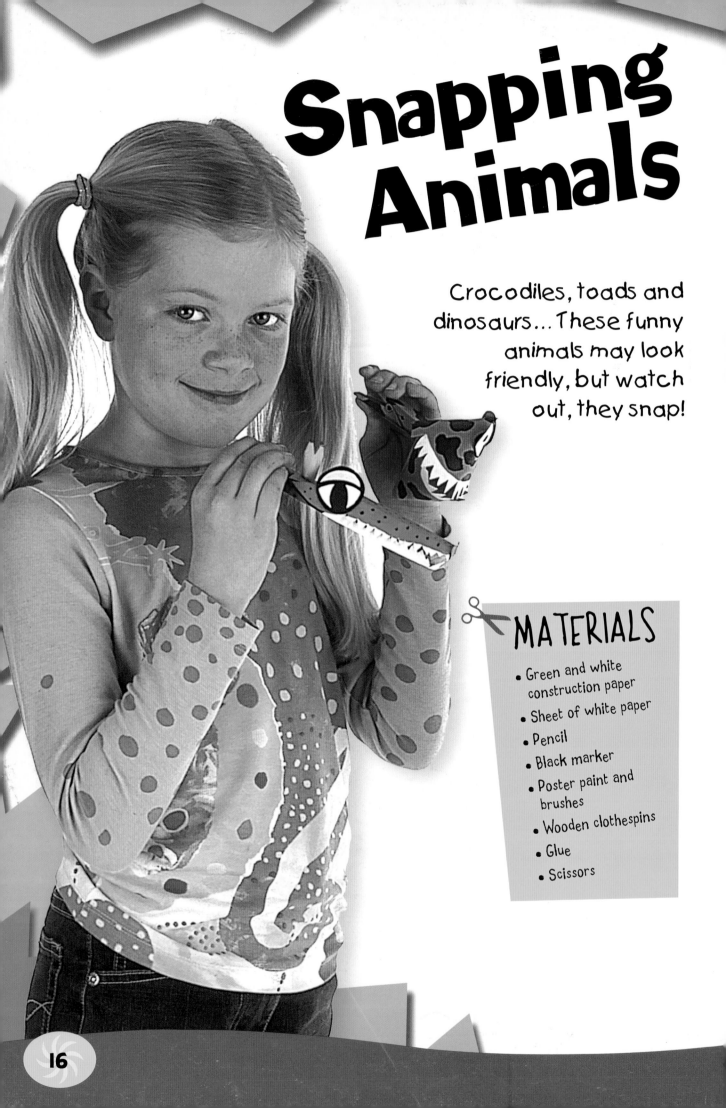

Snapping Animals

Crocodiles, toads and dinosaurs... These funny animals may look friendly, but watch out, they snap!

MATERIALS

- Green and white construction paper
- Sheet of white paper
- Pencil
- Black marker
- Poster paint and brushes
- Wooden clothespins
- Glue
- Scissors

Make sure your
clothespins are very
clean before you
paint them.
Be sure to use
wooden clothespins,
not plastic.

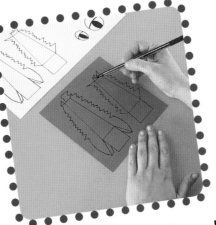

Copy the jaw's template, shown at right, onto green construction paper. Cut out the pieces.

1

2

Fold the green pieces to form the crocodile's jaws.

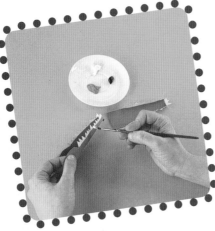

3

Paint the teeth white.

4

Paint the clothespin green and let dry. Glue the jaws to the closed ends of the clothespin.

5

Draw the eyes in black marker, cut them out and glue them on.

HINT
Make sure the paint is dry before you put the pieces together and glue them on. Add a drop of glue to the tip of the clothespin, wait a minute, then add another drop before you attach the jaw to it.

JAWS TEMPLATE

Foam Animals

This funny zebra and silly giraffe are easy to make out of poster board paper and foam. Take them outside to play on the grass or decorate your room with them.

1 Fold a piece of poster board in half. Draw the zebra's body on one half. Draw the head and tail on a separate piece of poster board. Use the picture below as a guide.

2 Fold the poster board for the body in half as shown. Cut out the body. Cut out the head and tail.

MATERIALS

- Poster board
- Craft foam sheets
- Scissors
- Glue
- Fine-tip black marker

3 Cut the stripes, muzzle, hooves, and teeth out of foam.

4 Glue the foam pieces onto the body, head and legs. Glue on the head and tail.

5 Unfold the board. Your animal will stand alone on its feet.

CAREFUL!
Not all glues work on foam. Choose a solvent-free glue that's made to use on plastic.

Spiral Snakes

These snakes make cool party decorations and take just minutes to make.

MATERIALS

- Construction paper in assorted colors
- Glue
- Scissors
- Black marker
- Thread and tape

1 Use a black marker to draw a spiral snake as shown.

2 Cut out the snake.

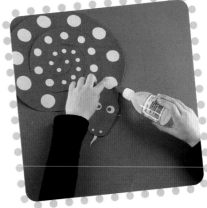

3

On a different sheet of colored paper, draw small shapes like circles or triangles to decorate your snake. Using the model as a guide, draw eyes, a tongue and nostrils. Cut out all the pieces.

4

Glue all the pieces onto your snake. Attach a long thread to make a hanging string.

BE A SNAKE CHARMER!
Hang up your spiral snake
and watch it twist in the air!

ARTISTIC CRAFTS

Splatter Painting

Spraying, splattering and splashing paint... this "drip technique" of painting was developed by American artist Jackson Pollock. It involves using a paintbrush to flick paint onto a canvas lying on the floor — without letting your brush touch the canvas!

MATERIALS

- Poster or acrylic paint
- Paintbrushes
- Old toothbrushes
- White drawing paper
- Black cardboard
- Ruler
- Pencil
- Scissors
- Art knife

1 Prepare your paint colors in bowls. Add enough water to make the paint thin and liquidy. Load a brush with paint.

2 Using Pollock's drip technique, spatter paint onto the paper by flicking the paintbrush at it.

3 You can also use a toothbrush. Dip it in paint and then spray the paper by running your finger across the bristles.

Make two drip paintings and let dry. On one, trace an edge half an inch wide around the border, then trace lines from top to bottom that are spaced 1 inch apart.

Cut strips to the lines, being careful not to cut the border.

On the other painting, trace and cut out strips that are 1 inch apart.

Take these strips and weave them in and out of the strips on the first painting.

Finish off your new work of art by pasting it onto black cardboard.

Paul Jackson Pollock was born in 1912 and died in 1956. During one of his trips across the country, Pollock discovered the "sand painting" technique of the Native Americans. He also was inspired by artists like Picasso, Miró, and Masson.

Optical Illusions

You can create amazing optical effects with just a sheet of paper and a marker. All you need to draw these geometric figures is a little patience.

Notice how you have a sense of a 3-D pyramid in the final drawing? Depending on how you look at it, the small square either seems to be down in the bottom of a hollow pyramid, or sitting at the top.

1 Draw a square. Mark each side: A on the left, B on the bottom, C on the top and D on the right.

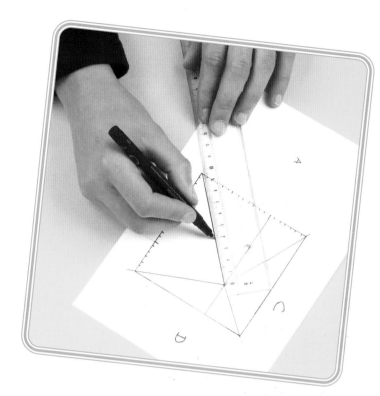

2 Draw a diagonal line across from corner AB to corner CD. Draw a diagonal line from corner BD toward the middle of side C, stopping where it meets the first diagonal line. Draw a diagonal line from corner AC to where it meets the other two lines.

3 Paint or color black stripes as shown. The stripes in sections A and B should be half an inch wide, and the stripes in sections C and D should be a quarter of an inch wide. Paint or color a small black square where all four lines intersect.

Look at the middle of the drawing on the right. Rotate the sheet slowly. As it turns, colors seem to appear before your eyes!

Chinese Painting

Discover the ancient technique of Chinese ink painting. Draw simple lines that you see in nature, as if you were writing in calligraphy. See how the ink and water flow into new shapes and shadings.

MATERIALS

- A special paintbrush for calligraphy
- A bowl of water
- Chinese ink
- A scrap of thick paper to test shadings
- Watercolor paper

1

Dilute a little Chinese ink in some water to make a light gray. Check its lightness by brushing it on a sheet of thick paper.

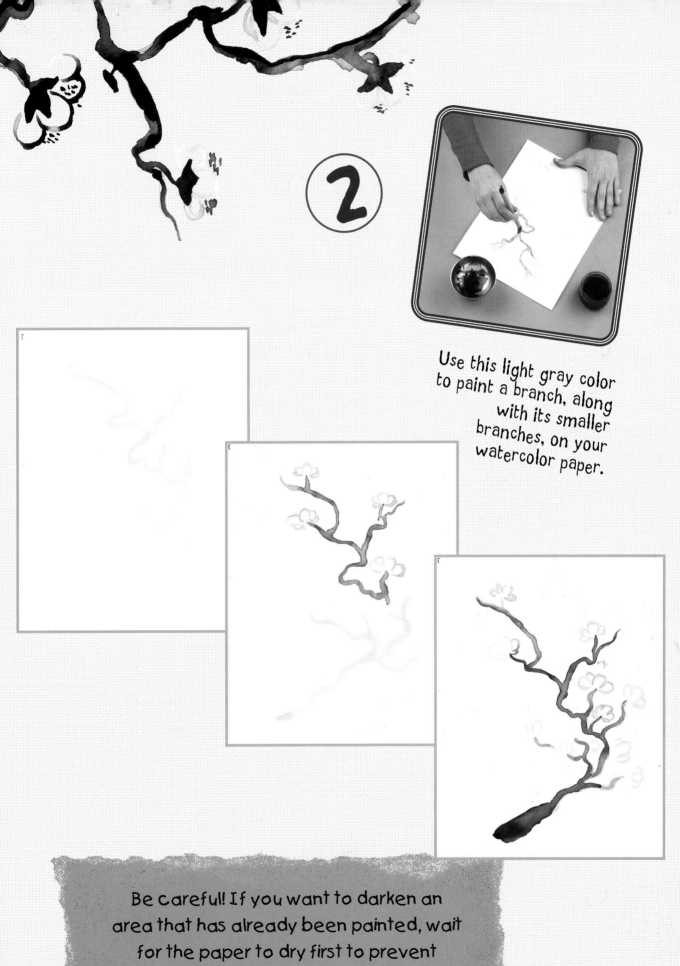

②

Use this light gray color to paint a branch, along with its smaller branches, on your watercolor paper.

Be careful! If you want to darken an area that has already been painted, wait for the paper to dry first to prevent smudging, then go over it again.

 **3**

Add more ink to the water to darken it. Outline the branch and add some shading, using downward strokes.

 **4**

Use black ink that is not diluted to add shadows and to make the base of the blooms.

 **5**

Paint the rest of the blooms in watered-down ink.

 **6**

Once you have mastered the technique, try painting a landscape. Be careful where you place your ink to create lighter and darker areas.

DID YOU KNOW?
The Chinese and Japanese art of writing with ink is known as calligraphy. Calligraphy means "beautiful writing."

33

CARDS

Bewitching Cards

The moon is up and the witches and bats are ready to fly! Here are some eye-catching cards to make for Halloween.

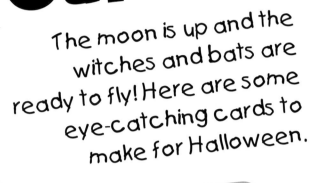

1

Cut a 6 inches square out of colored construction paper.

2

Draw your design (a witch, bat, moon or star) and cut it out with an art knife.

✂ MATERIALS

- Orange, violet and black construction paper
- Black and orange raffia
- Large embroidery needle
- Hole punch
- Scissors
- Art knife
- Ruler
- Pencil
- Glue

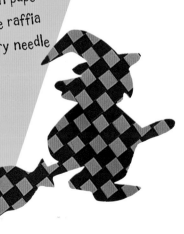

3

Cut a 5 inches square out of black construction paper. Measure and cut strips that are half an inch wide, being careful to stop half an inch before the edge of the construction paper.

4

Measure and cut strips of construction paper that are 6 inches long by half an inch wide in a different color. Cut them out.

6

Lay the construction paper with your cutout design on top of the black construction paper. Use a hole punch to make a hole every half inch around the edge. Thread a strand of raffia through the holes and tie it into a bow at the end.

5

Weave these strips in and out of the black construction paper as shown.

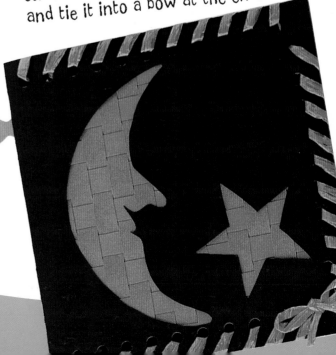

Heart Notebook

You can keep precious souvenirs, notes, and photos in this heart-shaped notebook.

MATERIALS

- 20 sheets of yellow paper
- 2 sheets of cardboard
- Yellow, red and white construction paper
- 2 metal key rings or paper fasteners
- Hole punch
- Glue
- Ribbon
- Pencil
- Small padlock

1

Put two pieces of cardboard together and cut out a large heart.

2

Fold 20 sheets of yellow paper in half to use as notebook filling. Make sure the paper will fit inside the heart covers. If not, trim the edges.

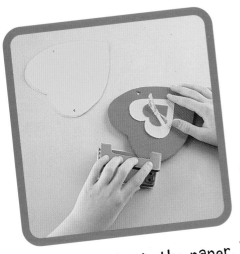

3

Punch two holes in the paper. Then punch two holes in the hearts that will line up with the paper.

4

With the paper between the hearts and all the holes matching up, attach the notebook together with two key rings or paper fasteners.

5

Decorate the cover with more hearts and ribbons.

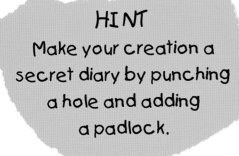

HINT
Make your creation a secret diary by punching a hole and adding a padlock.

You can make a rectangular notebook, too!

Japanese Kimono Cards

Fold origami paper into a series of beautiful Japanese kimono cards.

✂ MATERIALS

- Origami paper
- Construction paper
- Pencil
- Black and red markers
- Glue
- Scissors
- Ruler

DID YOU KNOW ?

The Japanese traditional clothing called a kimono is made of only one piece of fabric.

1

Fold a sheet of origami paper along the vertical lines, and then along the diagonal lines as shown at right.

2

Draw the face, hands and feet on colored construction paper and cut them out. Draw the wig on black paper and cut it out.

3

Draw the eyes and nose with a black marker. Use a red marker to draw the mouth.

4

Glue all the pieces onto a sheet of colored cardboard folded in two to make a card.

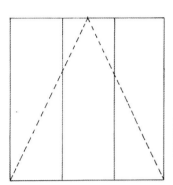

On the back of the square sheet of origami paper, use a ruler to trace two vertical lines that will divide the sheet into three equal sections. Trace a triangle from the top center point of the paper down to the bottom corners.

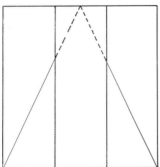

Cut along the two diagonal lines that are colored blue in the diagram. Do not cut the part where the lines are dotted.

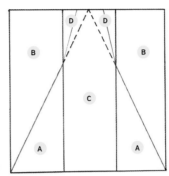

Write letters on each section as shown. Fold A over C toward the center. Fold B over D toward the outside. Fold B diagonally toward the back (following the blue lines on the diagram).

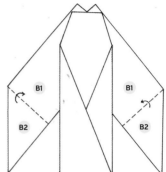

Fold B2 over B1 along the dotted lines.

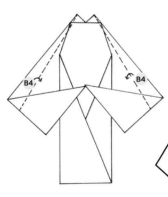

Fold B4 toward the inside along the dotted lines.

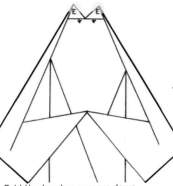

Fold the two top corners down.

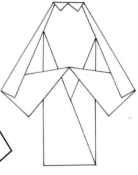

Turn the kimono over. This is the front of the kimono.

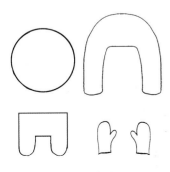

GAME CRAFTS

The Wiggling Nose

Pointy or twisted, wiggling or stretching... transform your character's nose with a wave of your hand!

MATERIALS

- White cardboard
- Colored construction paper
- Pencil
- Black marker
- Scissors
- Black beads
- Black thread
- Glue
- Poster paint

1
Draw your character's profile, skipping the nose, on white cardboard.

Shake your picture gently to make hundreds of funny faces!

2 String a bunch of black beads on a 4- to 5-inch long thread.

3 Punch a hole at the top and at the bottom of your profile. Pass the ends of the thread through the holes and tape them at the back.

You can make a rectangular frame instead, if you like. Hold the frame flat, tip it slowly and watch your character's nose come to life!

The Frame

2 Lay it on your drawing, trace the outline, and then cut off the excess paper. Paint your frame and decorate it with paper cut-outs or stickers.

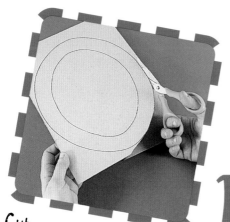

1 Cut an oval frame out of white cardboard.

3 Glue the frame to your drawing. Glue another sheet of cardboard to the back of your drawing to hide the threads.

Cartoon Book

Funny faces, bizarre bodies, and laughable legs... These cartoon characters change before your eyes — all you have to do is turn the pages!

1

Stack three sheets of paper on top of one another. Fold them into three equal sections across the widest part of the paper.

2

Use the ruler to divide the sheets into three equal sections across the narrower part of the paper. Mark off the sections in pencil.

3

Draw a funny cartoon character in the middle section. The head should be in the top part, the body in the middle and the legs in the bottom section.

4

Cut through all the paper along your pencil lines. Do not cut the middle section.

5

Fold over one section at a time and draw a head, body, and legs for other characters, until all the pages are full.

6

Your book is done. All you have to do is turn the pages in different combinations to discover new cartoon characters.

Draw Your Own Maze

Have fun drawing a picture that has a maze built into it. A maze is a path with one entrance, one exit, a few crossroads... and many dead ends! Can you get lost in it? Of course, but you're the designer of this ingenious and mysterious game!

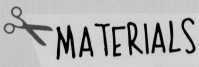

MATERIALS

- A sheet of white paper
- Black markers

1

Draw the general outline of the maze picture in pencil. You can use this clown's head as an example, if you like.

2

Retrace the lines in black marker. Be careful not to cross the lines and to leave open paths in different areas of the drawing, for example, in the nose, mouth and eyes.

3

In each area, draw little mazes with an entrance and exit.

4

Fill in the empty spaces with more paths and draw the main entrance. In this example, it's under the chin.

5

Try tracing a path through your maze with a pencil and make sure you can get out! Imagine the mazes you can design inside other pictures.

DID YOU KNOW?

The earliest maze was described in an ancient Greek myth. The maze was home to the dreaded minotaur, a monster that was half-man, half-bull. Theseus defeated the minotaur and found his way out of the maze. The Romans often decorated the floors of their villas with maze designs of mosaic tile. Some city parks feature giant mazes made from hedges.

49

Silly Face People

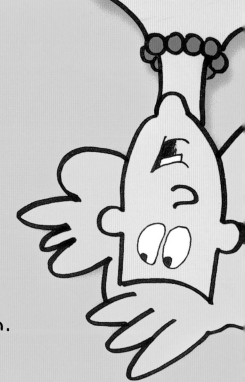

A sly glance, a smile, a scowl, or funny face... You can change the expressions on your characters in the blink of an eye by sliding the strips of paper behind them.

MATERIALS

- Drawing paper
- Pencil
- Black and colored markers
- Ruler
- Glue
- Scissors
- Art knife

1

Fold a sheet of drawing paper in two like a book. Draw your character's head on the "front cover." Trace a rectangle where the eyes should be and another rectangle at the mouth.

2

Unfold the sheet. Make two cuts along the fold, at the same height as the eye and mouth sections. Cut out the two rectangles.

3

Cut two long strips of paper the same width as the rectangles you've cut out. On one strip draw different sets of eyes, and on the other draw different kinds of mouths.

4

Slide the strips of paper through the cuts in the fold. Fold the sheet closed and hold it in place with a few drops of glue. Now slide the eyes and mouth and see all the silly faces you can make.

Dragon Fortune-teller

Dragons are a symbol of wisdom. See what this fun game has in store for you.

MATERIALS

- 2 sheets of paper
- Pencil
- Markers
- Scissors

1

Fold a sheet of square paper in half, corner to corner, to make a triangle. Fold the triangle in half to make another triangle. Unfold the sheet. Fold the four corners so that they meet perfectly in the center to form a square. Keep the sheet folded and turn it over. Fold all four corners into the center again. Fold the square in half to make a rectangle, and in half again to make a small square. Unfold it back to a rectangle. Slip your thumbs and index fingers into the four compartments underneath. This is how you will make the fortune-teller move.

2

Use our model to help you draw the dragon face on the outside of the fortune-teller. Color it in with markers.

3

Draw, color and cut out the dragon's horns, beard, and crest.

4

Glue the pieces onto the dragon as shown in the photo.

5

Write a message in each of the compartments. Ask your friend to name a number. Move the fortune-teller with your fingers to count to that number. Have your friend pick a flap. Open the compartment to read the message inside.

Optical Illusions
Spinning Disks

Here are some optical illusions that are sure to make your head spin! Observe the differences between the two spirals and the sensation you get from each one as you watch it in motion...

On this drawing, there are two spirals, one inside the other. When you spin the disk, they seem to move in two directions at once.

On this drawing, there is only one kind of spiral. When you spin the disk, the spiral seems to move outward.

MATERIALS

- Photocopier
- Paper
- White cardboard
- Glue
- Scissors
- Paper clips

1 Use a photocopier to copy the two spirals shown here (or you can trace them). Cut out the photocopied spirals.

2 Cut two circles out of cardboard.

3 Glue your spiral onto the cardboard.

4 Straighten out a paper clip and stick one end into the back of the spiral disk at its center point.

5 Hold the paper clip between your hands. Rub your hands together to make the spiral spin and see what happens!

GIFT CRAFTS

Seashell Characters

Make these funny and original characters out of seashells from the beach or craft store.

✂ **MATERIALS**

- 2 large wide seashells (for the body)
- 2 smaller flat shells (for the feet)
- 2 round shells (for the eyes)
- 1 shell for the nose
- Self-hardening modeling clay
- Colored plastic-coated wire
- Scissors
- Paint and paintbrush

1 Use modeling clay to fit the two large shells together. Cover the open edges at the back of the shells with clay.

2 Use the modeling clay or glue to stick two shells to the top for the eyes and nose.

Use the modeling clay
to stick two shells to
the bottom for the feet.

3

4

Cut a piece of wire. Bend
two of the wire ends into
hands. Stick the wire into
the clay holding the body
together near the back.

5

Paint the body, eyes and arms
in a bright color. When dry,
paint a stripe around the edge
of the body.

6

Paint the nose red.
Paint the feet black,
the irises of the eyes
white and the pupils black
as shown.

Fabric Wall Hangings

Scraps of fabric can be turned into pretty wall hangings to give as gifts.

MATERIALS

- Fabric in an assortment of colors and patterns
- Felt
- Repositionable glue or fabric glue
- Scissors
- Pinking shears
- Fine-tip marker
- Ruler

1

Measure a rectangle 15 inches by 18 inches on a piece of fabric.

2

Cut it out with pinking shears so the ends don't fray.

3

Cut different shapes out of other pieces of fabric. Choose fabrics and colors that look nice together.

4

Glue your pieces onto the rectangle. You can layer them to make different designs.

HINT
Using this technique, you can create an entire scene out of different fabrics, such as this lovely house.

Butterfly Pencil Holder

Collect empty spaghetti boxes to make these pencil holders. You can decorate your wall with them!

MATERIALS

- Empty spaghetti box
- Bristol board
- Mini envelopes
- Colored plastic-covered wire or pipe cleaners
- Small balls
- Paint and paintbrushes
- Scissors
- Glue
- Large, fat nail
- Pens and pencils
- Paper clips

1 Draw the wings on bristol board. Cut them out and paint them.

Cut two mini envelopes in half, glue them to the wings, and paint them. Keep open ends of envelopes at top.

3 Cut out a "mouth" into the front and sides of the spaghetti box. Paint the box. Pierce two holes at the top as shown. Curl two pipe cleaners around your finger. Insert the pipe cleaners into the top of the box and glue them in place.

4 Make 12 holes all the way through the sides using the large nail.

5 Cut eyes and pupils out of bristol board. Paint them and glue them on.

6 Glue the butterfly body onto the wings. Stick paper or foam balls onto the ends of the pipe cleaners and glue them in place.

Felt-covered Notebooks

For a fun school year, why not cover your notebooks in soft felt? Decorate them with animals to keep you company all day long!

MATERIALS

- Felt in assorted colors
- Scissors
- White glue
- Pencil
- Notebook

1

Cut out a large piece of felt in the same dimensions as your notebook, adding 1 inch extra for flaps to wrap around the sides. Glue the felt onto the cover of your notebook.

2

Fold the flaps and glue them inside the cover.

3

Draw the pieces for your animal on assorted pieces of felt.

4

Cut out each piece of felt.

5

Assemble the pieces to make the animal and then glue it onto the cover.

6

Cut a strip of felt that is 2 inches long and half an inch wide. Glue it onto the cover to hold your pen or pencil.

MASKS

African Ceremonial Masks

Ceremonial masks, warrior masks, masks for celebrations — African art is rich in abstract design. Using our model for inspiration, make an exotic mask out of cardboard, paper, and glue that is sure to impress your friends.

Masks have often figured in traditional African ceremonies and in theater. These kinds of masks would usually be made of clay or wood and decorated in plant fibers.

MATERIALS

- Cardboard
- Paper towel
- Glue
- Pencil
- Paint
- Paintbrushes
- Scissors or art knife

Copy the shape of the mask on cardboard. Draw two large circles in the middle for the eyes.

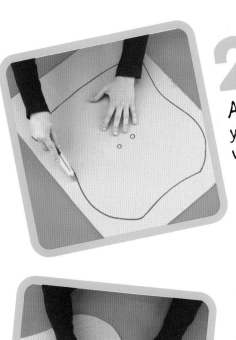

2

Ask a grown-up to help you cut out the mask with the art knife.

3

Roll sheets of paper towel between your hands to make strings.

4

Glue the strings onto the mask to decorate the face. Make sure the glue is dry before you start painting.

5

Paint the base color. Paint the eyes and the rest of the features in other colors.

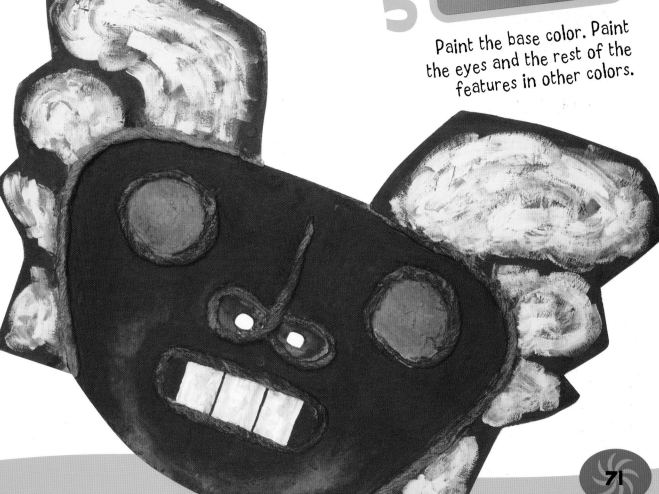

Paper Wig

With this elegant wig you'd be right at home in a British courtroom...or even the court of a French king! All you need are a lot of white paper and some patience.

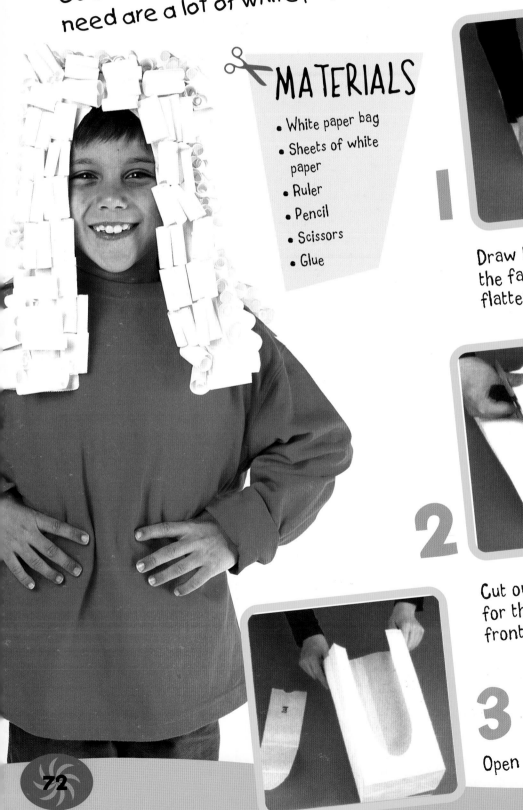

MATERIALS

- White paper bag
- Sheets of white paper
- Ruler
- Pencil
- Scissors
- Glue

1

Draw the opening for the face on a flattened paper bag.

2

Cut out the opening for the face on the front of the bag.

3

Open the bag.

4 Cut white paper into strips 4 inches wide by 10 inches long.

5 Roll the strips of paper around a pencil or your finger to make them curl.

6 Glue the paper curls onto the bag one by one. Start at the sides.

7 Alternate the direction of the curls and don't make the rows too straight. This will give the wig more volume.

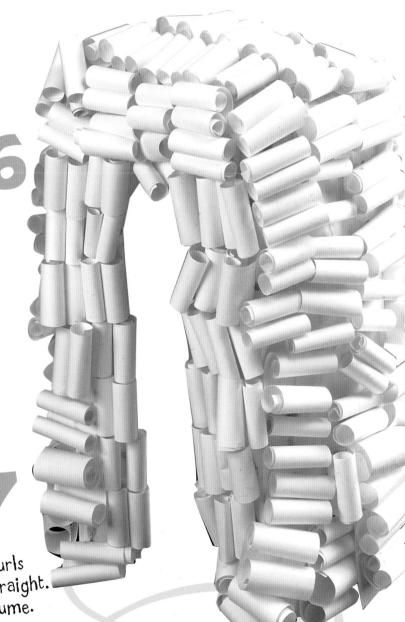

Collage Masks

Cut photos of animals, fruits, or plants out of magazines and make outrageous collage masks reminiscent of the style of Italian artist Guiseppe Arcimboldo.

MATERIALS

- Magazines or catalogs
- Construction paper
- Pencil
- Scissors
- Stapler
- Glue
- Elastic band

Cut a large face out of a magazine. This will be the base of your mask. Draw a curved line on the face so that the mouth and jaw are below the line. Cut off the lower part of the face.

2 Cut photos of your favorite objects in different sizes and colors out of a magazine or catalog.

3 Glue the mask onto the sheet of paper. Arrange the animals above the eyes and glue them on in layers.

4 Cut off the extra paper at the top of the mask.

5 Cut out the eyes in the mask. Pierce a hole on each side of the mask, pass the ends of the elastic band through the holes and knot them in place.

Plank Mask

African plank masks are used in rituals to frighten off enemies. Its imposing size and mysterious look will impress your friends as you dance a traditional ritual dance!

1

Taking inspiration from the example shown here, draw the mask on a large sheet of cardboard. Make it tall!

2

On another piece of cardboard, draw the decorative pieces to be cut out and glued: circles for the eyes, squares and triangles for the rest of the face.

MATERIALS

- Corrugated cardboard
- Pencil
- All-purpose glue
- Scissors
- Paint and paintbrushes
- Raffia
- Adhesive tape

COLORS AND SYMBOLS

The African craftsman finds his colors in nature. White comes from kaolin, a type of clay. Black comes from charcoal, and red comes from ochre, which is earth that contains iron ore. The mask reproduced on this page was inspired by a mask from the African nation, Burkina Faso.

3

Apply a thick layer of white paint over the entire surface of the mask. Let it dry, then draw a geometric design on it. Paint the black parts of the design.

4

Paint a cardboard rectangle red. Fold it in two and glue it on for a nose. Paint the other decorative elements you have prepared and glue them on as well.

DID YOU KNOW?
A mask did not have any special powers until it was used in a public ritual for the first time. Before such a ceremony, no special precautions had to be taken in handling the mask. Afterward, it was another story....

5

Use adhesive tape to attach long strands of raffia to the back of your mask. Pierce two holes for the eyes and hide behind your mask to wait for the enemy!

WORLD CRAFTS

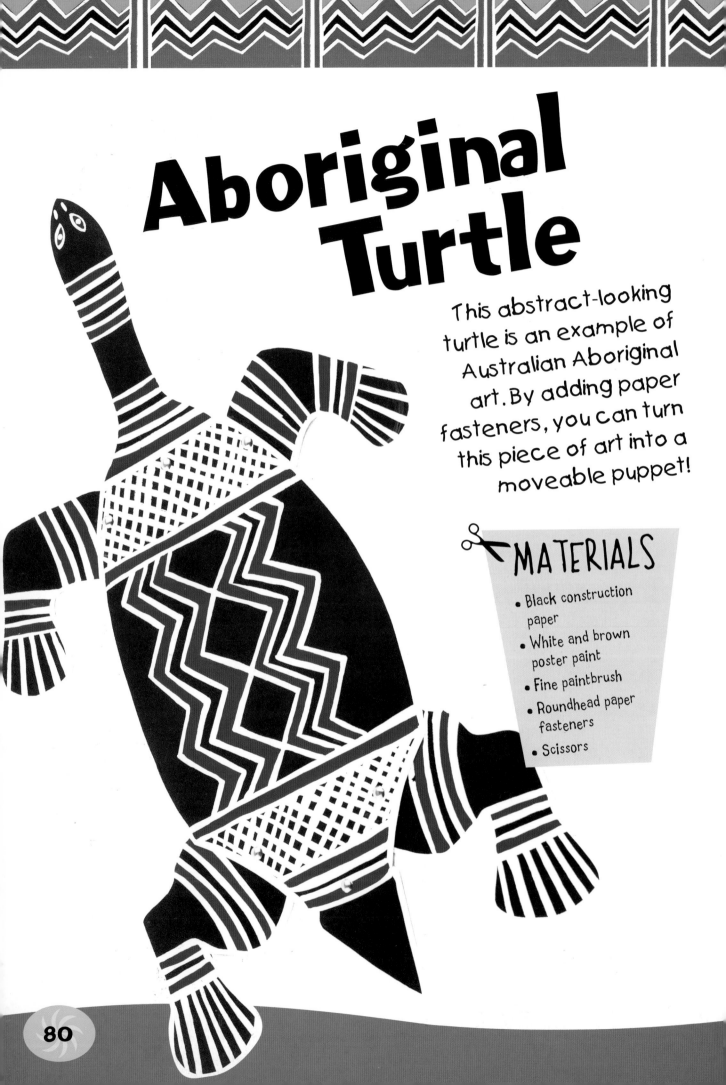

Aboriginal Turtle

This abstract-looking turtle is an example of Australian Aboriginal art. By adding paper fasteners, you can turn this piece of art into a moveable puppet!

MATERIALS

- Black construction paper
- White and brown poster paint
- Fine paintbrush
- Roundhead paper fasteners
- Scissors

1 Draw the turtle's body, head, and legs on black paper. Outline the different shapes in white paint.

2 Carefully cut out all the pieces.

3 Using our model for inspiration, draw geometric designs on the pieces and paint them brown and white.

4 Attach the turtle's head and legs with paper fasteners.

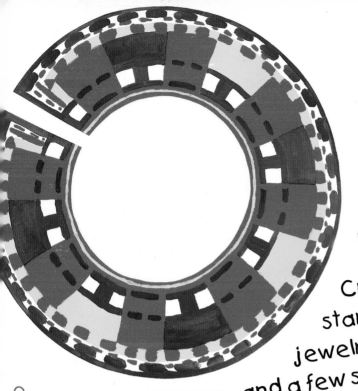

World Jewelry

Create a fun costume by starting with Egyptian and African jewelry. All you need is a little paint and a few scraps of paper or cardboard to make this necklace.

MATERIALS

- Construction paper
- Poster paint and paintbrushes
- Compass
- Art knife
- Scissors

African Necklace

1 Draw a 24-inch circle. Inside it draw a smaller 14-inch circle.

2 Cut out the outer circle with scissors and then the inner circle using the art knife or scissors.

3 Draw designs on your necklace and then paint them. You can find inspiration in African fabrics or in pictures of Africa.

4 Let your necklace dry and then cut out a half inch piece from it so you can slip it around your neck.

Egyptian Necklace

1 Paint a strip of cardboard. Choose a color like brown.

✂ **MATERIALS**

- Corrugated cardboard
- Poster paint
- Paintbrushes
- Scissors
- Black yarn
- Large needle
- Large colored beads

2 Cut out diamonds 4 inches long and 1 inch wide, as well as little triangles.

3 Using the needle and a 24-inch length of yarn, string the diamonds and triangles as shown.

4 Add a second string, alternating diamonds with beads (tie knots to hold them in place). Tie all the ends together.

Dragon Puppets

Have fun making these colorful dragons, and then watch them come to life in your hands! Why not put on a show with your friends — and make the puppets dance.

MATERIALS

- Square box
- Styrofoam balls, large and small
- Paint in assorted colors
- Paintbrushes
- Glue
- Paper streamers
- Red and white lightweight felt
- Art knife
- Scissors
- Glue stick

DID YOU KNOW?
In China, dragons symbolize the Emperor. The dragon also represents heavenly and creative power, as well as authority to the Chinese.

1

Cut the square box on three sides only and fold it.

2

Apply an undercoat of white paint over the entire box. Allow it to dry.

3

Paint the box black inside, and another color outside.

4

Cut the streamers into long strips of different sizes to make the puppet's tail.

5

Cut the large Styrofoam ball in half to make the eyes, and then paint the pupils black.

6

Glue the streamers to the box using the glue stick.

7

Glue on the eyes. Cut out the teeth and a long tongue from the felt. Glue them on.

8

Paint the small Styrofoam ball red and glue it on for the nose.

Totem Pole

The native people of the Pacific Northwest carved totem poles that told stories. Why not make up your own animal legend and build a miniature totem out of paper?

1

Draw a rectangle that's the length of the cardboard tube and 6 inches wide. Draw and cut out strips of lighter colored paper in assorted widths.

2

Glue the strips of paper onto the rectangle.

3

Wrap the rectangle around the cardboard tube and glue it in place.

4

Draw the different pieces for your totem characters on colored paper.

Outline the pieces in black paint and cut them out.

5

6

Assemble your characters by gluing the different pieces together.

7

Glue your characters onto the cardboard tube.

Accordion Fish

A Japanese celebration wouldn't be complete without fans made to look like fish. Accordion pleated and mounted on sticks, they move in interesting ways!

MATERIALS

- Colored construction paper
- Glitter glue pens
- Markers
- Pencil
- Wooden skewers
- Glue
- Scissors

1 Copy our fish model onto a large sheet of construction paper.

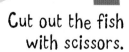

2 Cut out the fish with scissors.

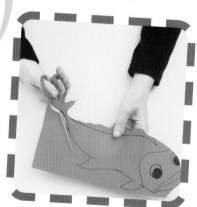

3 Draw the fish's scales and decorate its face with the glitter glue pen.

4 Glue the wood skewers to the back of the fish, one at the head and one near the tail.

5 Fold the body of the fish into accordion pleats.

DID YOU KNOW?
In Japan, the fish is a symbol of courage.

Kimono Painting

Long ago in Japan, during the Samurai era, the kimono was a true work of art that families handed down from one generation to the next. The form of the garment, its fabric, colors, and patterns made it as valuable as a painting.

MATERIALS

- A roll of solid-colored wrapping paper or other designer paper
- Pencil, ruler
- Scissors, glue
- Paint and paintbrushes

1

Unroll the paper and trace the different parts of the kimono on it: the body, the sleeves, the collar and the belt, or obi.

2

Cut out each piece.

3

Glue the sleeves to the back of the body.

4

Fold the collar and glue it to the front of the body.

5

Decorate the kimono by painting flowers, leaves or other designs inspired by nature.

DID YOU KNOW?
The word kimono comes from the words ki, which means "to wear," and mono, which means "thing." This traditional Japanese garment is made of silk, cotton, or linen. Women's kimonos, which come in brighter colors than the men's, are wrapped in a wide belt called the obi. The obi may be 13 feet long. It is tied at the back with a knot, called the obiage, and a small cord, called the obijime. The wide sleeves can be used as pockets.

6

Paint the obi a different color and glue it to the front of the kimono. Hang your artwork on the wall. Dream up other costumes to make in new patterns!

Chinese Dragon

In China, there are dragons of every shape and color! A symbol of energy and a bright future, the Chinese dragon is a part of many celebrations. Make it dance, or run with it and watch its mane blow in the wind!

1

Draw the dragon's head on the drawing paper and cut it out. Trace the head on the yellow tissue paper and cut it out.

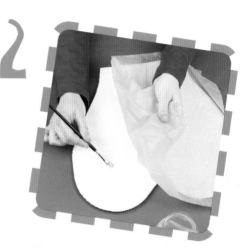

2

Glue the yellow shape to the dragon's head.

Bend the lid and glue it to the box so that the dragon's mouth remains partly open. Paint the box yellow. Then glue the head to the back of the box.

3

MATERIALS

- Shoebox
- Sheet of stiff drawing paper
- Large Styrofoam ball
- Red, green, and yellow tissue paper
- Paint
- Paintbrush
- Scissors
- Glue

4

Cut narrow strips in multiple layers of red tissue paper and glue them on the head and sticking out from under the box.

5

Cut narrow strips of green paper and wide strips of yellow paper, then glue them to the back of the head. Cut the Styrofoam ball in two to make a pair of eyes, draw pupils on them with a black marker and glue the eyes onto the head.

6

Add long strips to make the tail.

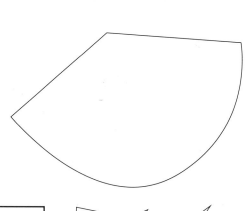

Babila and the Sorcerer

Storytelling is a celebrated tradition throughout Africa. Songs, poems, and stories have been carried down year after year through the spoken word. Perhaps, you will make up some stories about Babila and the Sorcerer and their "Little African Village."

Pieces for the Sorcerer

1

Cut the feet and arms out of brown paper. Form a cone with the yellow construction paper and glue it together with the glue stick. Use the template as a guide.

2

Cut a small rectangle of yellow paper and glue it into a larger rectangle of brown paper. Cut the edges of the brown paper to make it jagged.

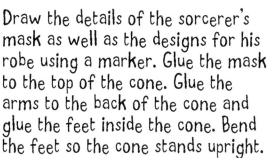

3

Draw the details of the sorcerer's mask as well as the designs for his robe using a marker. Glue the mask to the top of the cone. Glue the arms to the back of the cone and glue the feet inside the cone. Bend the feet so the cone stands upright.

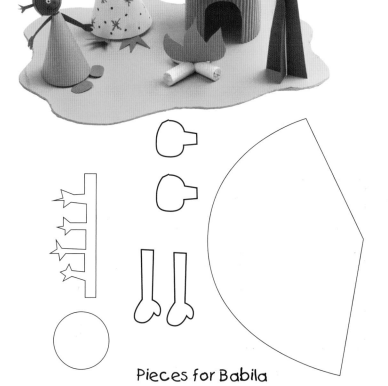

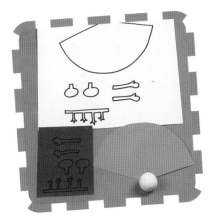

4

Do the same for the Babila character, but cut a circle for the head and paint it brown.

Pieces for Babila

Little African Village

This little village sets the perfect scene for many stories starring Babila and the Sorcerer.

MATERIALS

- Construction paper
- Thin wood, twigs, or straw
- Kraft paper
- Glue stick
- Scissors
- Markers
- Paint

1

Copy the different shapes on colored paper and cut them out. Use brown paper for the tree and its base, green for the leaves, orange for the flames, and light brown for the roof of the house.

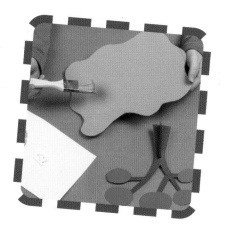 

2 Cut the shape of the ground out of cardboard and paint yellow. Glue the leaves of the tree onto the branches. Make a slit in the trunk and in the base to fit them together. This cross-shape will help the tree stand up.

 **3**

Make a cone-shaped roof out of the kraft paper, glue it together and cut a fringe around the edge with the scissors. Cut the house out of corrugated cardboard, glue it into a cylinder shape and place the roof on top.

Cut three pieces of balsa wood—two small and one larger. Consider breaking a twig instead or cutting a straw into three pieces. Glue the two small pieces to either side of the larger piece to make a cross. Fold the flames at the base to make a tab and glue them to the balsa wood cross.

 **4**

Egyptian Frescoes

Paint a scene from everyday life in the land of the pharaohs. These scenes appear on the frescoes that decorated the tombs of the ancient kings and queens. Choose the kinds of colors that were used on the frescoes, like ochre, brown, blue and white. These resemble natural pigments that came from the earth and rocks.

MATERIALS

- Construction paper
- Glue stick
- Scissors
- Markers

Looking at pictures of Egyptian frescoes for inspiration, draw your designs in black marker, filling in all the spaces on your paper. Our model shows pillars decorated with vegetables, animals, and a hunter with a bow and arrow.

A word of advice: Draw your characters in profile, and keep your shapes simple.

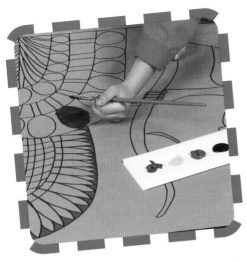

Think of other scenes from daily life in ancient Egypt, like fishermen in a rowboat on the Nile, dancers, or servants bringing offerings to the pharaoh.

2 Paint the designs, choosing harmonizing colors. Let the paint dry well.

3

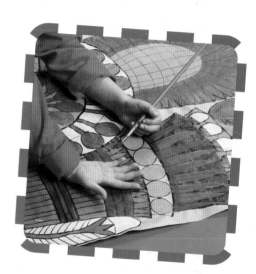

Use the black marker to outline the designs again, if necessary. This will make them stand out.

HOLIDAY CRAFTS

Christmas Wreaths

MATERIALS

- Brown corrugated cardboard
- Red, green and dark green corrugated cardboard
- Paper or small foam balls
- Red ribbon
- Gold string
- Green and red paint
- Paintbrushes
- Toothpicks
- Pencil
- Scissors
- Art knife
- Glue

A holiday wreath on your door sends out warm "season's greetings!" You can welcome friends with two types of homemade wreaths.

1

Draw a 12-inch diameter circle on the brown cardboard. Draw a 6-inch diameter circle inside it. Cut out the larger circle. Ask a grown-up to cut out the smaller circle with the art knife.

2

Paint one side with a thick coat of dark green paint. Let dry.

You can also paint small boxes in holiday colors, tie ribbons around them and attach to the wreath. Follow the example at right.

3

Draw and cut a holly leaf out of cardboard. Use it to trace about 24 leaves in dark green and light green cardboard. Cut them out.

4

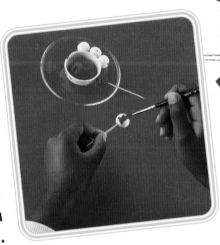

Paint the balls red. Stick them onto toothpicks or straight pins to make them easier to paint.

5

Glue the leaves onto the wreath, overlapping them and alternating colors as shown.

6

Glue on the red balls. Cut the red ribbon into 20-inch lengths, tie into bows and glue onto the wreath. Glue a loop of gold string onto the back of the wreath so you can hang it.

Santa's Reindeer

Santa has nine reindeer to pull his sleigh full of gifts. How many can you make?

① Copy the head, body, feet, neck and tail pieces as shown onto foam board. Have an adult cut the pieces out. Use them to trace three more sets of pieces.

MATERIALS

- Foam board
- Foam balls in two sizes (4 larger, 8 smaller)
- Red, green, yellow, orange, and blue crepe paper
- Red, green, yellow, orange and blue paint
- Paintbrushes
- Pencil
- Art knife
- Scissors
- Thin metal wire
- Toothpicks or straight pins
- Twigs

106

Paint the pieces yellow, red, green, orange, and blue as shown.

THE REINDEER GAME

The Reindeer Game is played by two to four players. You will need a dice. Each number in the dice corresponds to a part of the reindeer:

1: Body
2: Front legs
3: Hind legs

4: Neck
5: Tail
6: Head

Each player chooses a different colored reindeer and lays the six pieces flat in front of them. The winner is the first to assemble the reindeer by rolling the dice to get all six numbers.

3 Paint four of the larger balls red for the noses. Stick them on toothpicks or straight pins to make them easier to paint. For the eyes, paint black pupils on eight small balls.

4 Cut notches in the neck, tail and feet pieces. Make a fringe for the tail out of crepe paper and slip it onto the tail. Paint twigs for the antlers.

5

Pierce the top of the head with a 2-inch piece of wire and wrap the ends around two antlers. Pierce another hole with a 1-inch piece of wire and insert two eyeballs onto the ends. Insert a 1/2-inch piece of wire into the front of the head and attach the nose the same way.

6

Fit together the rest of the pieces as shown. You can tilt the head and tail in different directions.

Egg Faces

Villains, clowns, movie stars... here are characters with plenty of personality! Why not try drawing some unusual faces on your eggs this Easter? These original table decorations are sure to delight your friends.

1

Apply a coat of white paint to the egg and let it dry. Paint color with irregular brushstrokes to give it some texture. Let it dry.

MATERIALS

- Hardboiled or Styrofoam eggs
- Poster paint in assorted colors
- Paintbrushes
- 12 inches of metal wire
- Large spool or small aluminum can

2

Draw the eyes, mouth, and nose of your character in pencil first.

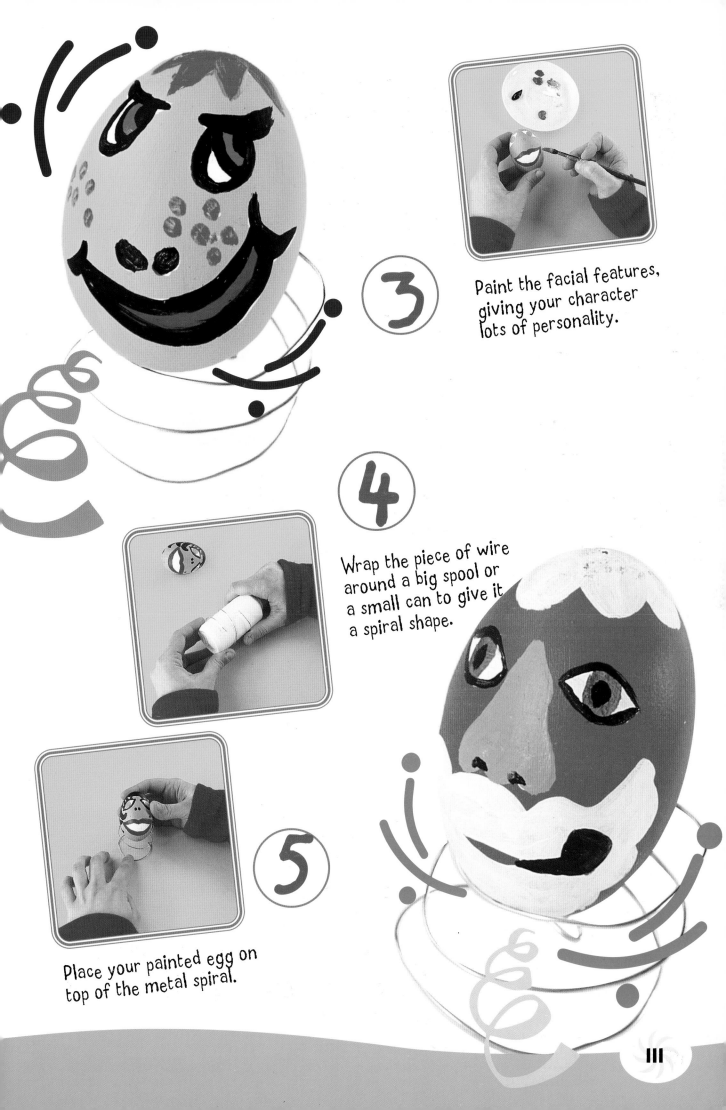

3 Paint the facial features, giving your character lots of personality.

4 Wrap the piece of wire around a big spool or a small can to give it a spiral shape.

5 Place your painted egg on top of the metal spiral.

Festive Placemats

Bring the entire henhouse to the table this Easter. Find inspiration in the color of spring to make these pretty placemats.

✂ MATERIALS

- Burlap (14 inches x 18 inches for each placement)
- Poster board
- Adhesive tape
- Pointy scissors or art knife
- Thick green yarn
- Large needle
- Straight pins
- Acrylic paint in assorted colors
- Paintbrush
- Steam iron

1 Cut a piece of burlap 14 inches wide by 18 inches long. Place a strip of adhesive tape around the edge of the fabric to keep it from fraying.

2

Cut a ½-inch diagonal slit in each corner. Fold each edge inward to make a hem. Use straight pins to hold the fabric in place. Ask a grown-up to iron the fabric to make it flat. Use the green yarn and needle to stitch the hem all around the placemat as shown. Remove the pins.

3 Cut squares out of board for the stencils. Trace your designs on them and cut them out with pointy scissors or an art knife.

4 Place your stencil on the placemat and paint over it. Make sure the paint is dry before you place another stencil close to it or use another color.

Salt Dough Lanterns

1

Prepare the salt dough. Flatten it out with a rolling pin on aluminum foil. Cut out Christmas tree shapes or star shapes. Stick a toothpick in the bottom of each tree or star. Punch little holes in them with a plastic straw.

Make a round flat dough base for your lantern. Place the metal holder of a tea light candle into the middle of the dough and press down slightly.

2

3

Stick the Christmas trees or stars into the dough base in a circle. Bake for one hour at 200°F.

To make salt dough, mix 2 cups of flour and 2 cups of salt with 1 cup of water.

4

After the lantern has cooled, paint it, let it dry, and put the tea light candle into its metal holder.

RECYCLE CRAFTS

Paper Houses

MATERIALS

- Shoe box, or large plastic beverage bottle for a round house
- Adhesive tape
- Assortment of paper (newspaper, gift wrap, etc.)
- Glue
- Heavy colored paper
- Scissors

Pink and round or multicolored and crooked, these houses are fun to make and totally original. Get together with your friends and create a whole city!

1 If using a shoe box, unfasten one end. Bend the two long sides inward and tape them down to give your house a funny shape.

3 Cut a door and windows out of heavy colored paper and glue them on your house.

2 Cover the box or plastic beverage bottle with paper. Use tape or glue to secure the paper.

4 Add other fun details, such as a roof, chimney, people at the windows, or a strip of grass at the bottom.

Tissue Box

A few strokes of the paintbrush, a pair of eyes, and some pipe cleaners are all it takes to turn an ordinary tissue box into an amazing creature!

To remove the tissues before painting the box, open the box carefully on one side and pull out the stack of tissues.

Characters

1
Carefully remove all the tissues from the box, then paint the box white.

2
After the paint has thoroughly dried, paint the box again, in a diffent color, leaving the area around the opening white. When dry, paint the area around the opening red to indicate a mouth.

Paint a black circle on each ball for the eyes.

Paint the plastic bottle cap black for the nose.

Twist the pipe cleaners into spirals and insert them into the top of the box for hair.

The undercoat of white paint hides the colors and writing on the box. If you don't give it this first coat, they will show through the colored paint.

Slide the stack of tissues back into the box and glue it closed. Glue on the eyes and nose.

Tissue Box Man

You can also turn your box into a person by adding a head, arms, and legs.

MATERIALS

- Box of tissues
- Heavy paper
- Poster paint
- Paintbrushes
- Toilet paper tubes
- Cork
- Glue
- Cotton balls

1 Cut two arms out of heavy paper, paint them, and glue them onto the top of the box.

2 Use toilet paper tubes to make the head and legs and a cork to make the nose. Paint them first, and then glue them on. Glue on some cotton balls for hair.

Crushed Aluminum Costume

Fold and crush disposable aluminum dishes and turn yourself into living art! Other famous artists have used this technique, including César, who made sculptures from compressed cars!

1

To make the smock, fold the fabric in two, trace a semicircle to mark where the neck will be, and cut it out. Do the same for the arms.

2

Sew the shoulders as shown in the photo.

MATERIALS

- Black open-weave or mesh fabric (about 5 feet long and wide enough to fit your body, or use an oversized T-shirt)
- Scissors
- Needle and thread
- Aluminum containers in assorted sizes (pie plates, take-out containers, etc.)
- Double-sided adhesive tape
- Plastic laces in assorted colors
- Elastic band (long enough to fit around your head comfortably)

3 Choose different kinds of disposable aluminum containers and flatten them with your feet or bend them into interesting shapes.

4 Carefully apply a piece of double-sided tape to the back of each aluminum piece.

If you aren't handy with a needle and thread, simply attach the aluminum dishes to an oversized T-shirt or sweatshirt.

5 Attach the pieces to your smock in an artistic way. Avoid the area under the arms. "Connect" the pieces with plastic laces. Attach a few pieces to the elastic for a hat, and tie around your head.

Spoon Puppets

Start with simple wooden spoons, stir in some colorful details... and you've got an amazing set of puppets! Picture a clown, a bumblebee, or maybe your own unique design for a funny insect. All this project calls for is a little imagination!

1 Paint the top of your wooden spoon yellow and let dry.

2 Paint black lines to make the bumblebee's stripes and let dry.

You can change your bumblebee's design by making the round part of the spoon its head and attaching a cardboard shape for the body.

3

Decorate with glitter glue to add sparkle and color.

4

Draw the wings on tissue paper and cut them out. Glue them to the sides of the body.

✂ MATERIALS

- Wooden spoon
- Paint and paintbrushes
- Glitter glue
- Pen or fine marker
- Colored tissue paper
- Scissors
- Glue
- Yellow and black construction paper
- Tiny black beads
- Small colored buttons
- Soft wire or plastic-coated wire

5

Cut a circle out of yellow construction paper. Draw a big smile on it, and make glittery cheeks. Glue on two black beads for eyes and a button for the nose.

6

Glue the head to the top of the body. For the antennae, wind two pieces of wire around your finger or a pen to give them a twisty shape. Glue little black paper circles to the end of each antenna. Glue the antennae to the back of the head.

7

Arrange the antennae at the top of the head, and your bumblebee is ready to fly.

129

City of the Future

Pretend you're an architect designing the city of the future! Combine different materials and original shapes to give it a three-dimensional look.

MATERIALS

- Scissors
- Corrugated cardboard
- Paper towel tubes
- Embellishments such as noodles, buttons, Baggie ties, tissue paper, etc.
- All-purpose glue
- Poster paint
- Paintbrushes

1

Use a large rectangle (or paper or cardboard) as the background for your city. Cut pieces of corrugated cardboard into various shapes and sizes.

2

Cut paper towel tubes lengthwise in half and then into a range of sizes. Assemble crumpled tissue paper and other items to add interest.

3

Using our model for inspiration, make your own city design on the background. Place the buildings and different elements onto the scene.

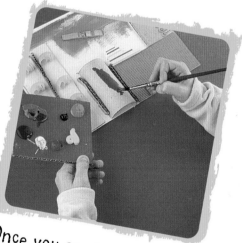

4

Once you are happy with the arrangement, glue each piece in place. Paint the pieces different colors, and glue on the extra details.

Look around your house for items such as paper clips, cotton balls, clothespins, tissue paper, erasers, Popsicle sticks, and the like. Add them to your buildings to create texture and added interest.

Easy String Puppets

MATERIALS

- 2 toilet paper tubes
- Hole punch
- Scissors
- Heavy colored paper
- Glue
- Red paint
- Paintbrushes
- Black marker
- Nylon thread
- Thick red string
- Raffia
- 3 wooden skewers or chopsticks
- Tape

Bright, bouncy, and easy to build, these puppets are sure to inspire hours of fun. Make up a story, put on a play, and watch them spring to life!

Puppets can be found on every continent and each country has its own techniques and traditions. In Europe and Africa, puppets hang from sticks and strings. In Southeast Asia, puppets make their mysterious appearance in the "shadow theater."

1

Use a hole punch to make four holes at each end of a toilet paper tube. This will be the body. Cut five rings from the second toilet paper tube, each about half an inch wide.

2

Paint the body roll and the five rings red.

3

Draw four ovals on yellow paper for the feet, a cone-shaped nose on orange paper, a heart-shaped head on red paper, and two circular eyes on white paper. Cut out the pieces.

Hint
Don't be shy about getting help! You can ask a friend to hold the pieces while you assemble them.

4

Glue the feet onto four of the red cardboard rings. Glue the base of the head to the fifth ring.

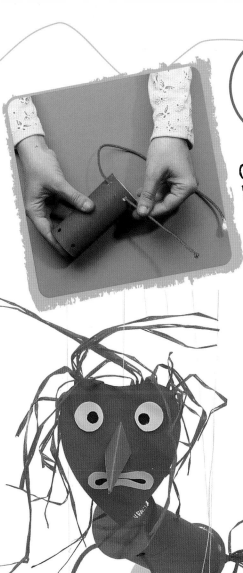

5

Cut some red string into two 5-inch lengths. Pass the strings through the holes at each end of the body and attach a paper foot to each end of the string.

6

Glue the nose, eyes, and mouth onto the head of your puppet. Make a tail and hair out of raffia.

Hint
You can use string instead of nylon thread. This will make your puppets more solid, especially if they are large.

7

Make a double cross out of the three wooden skewers or chopsticks, and glue them together.

8

Cut two red circles out of paper. Pass the red string through them to attach the head and tail to the body. Attach the legs, head, and tail to the wooden cross with nylon thread.

Lollipop Costume

This party costume gets its inspiration from giant multicolored lollipops. This candy store classic is fun to wear and still leaves you free to dance!

1

Make a small circle out of corrugated cardboard for a hat.

2

Cut out the circle, and then cut some long, thin strips of cardboard.

3

Roll up the strips and glue them in a spiral to the cardboard circle. Let dry.

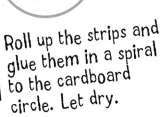

4 Paint the hat in bright contrasting colors.

Make two holes, one on each side of the hat. Pass a string through the holes so you can tie it on.

5

6

Cut out two large cardboard circles for the lollipop "body." Glue on long strips of cardboard in spirals, the same way you did for the hat. Paint with bright colors. Make two holes near the top of each circle. Pass string through the holes to attach the two circles, with the string resting over your shoulders.

Paper Plate Puppets

Paper plates do more than serve up food!
With a little paint and lots of imagination,
you can turn them into slimy creatures!

MATERIALS
- Paper plates
- Heavy paper
- Pencil and ruler
- Scissors
- Thick black marker
- Poster paint
- Paintbrushes
- Metal paper fasteners

Some paper plates have a thin coating on the top that makes them waterproof and keeps paint from sticking. If you are using this kind, you will have to paint them on the uncoated side.

1

Use a pencil and ruler to draw a line across the back of the plate, dividing it into a larger section and a smaller one.

2

Carefully cut the plate, following the line you drew.

3

Paint the underside of both pieces the same color. Then add polka dots, stripes, or other designs. Let dry.

To make wiggly legs for your creature, cut out strips of thin cardboard and fold them accordion-style. Attach them to the body with paper fasteners.

4 Draw legs, eyes, and other details for your character on heavy paper and outline them in black marker.

5 Glue the eyes to the smaller piece of plate, and then attach this piece to the larger piece.

6 Attach the arms and legs with metal paper fasteners.

Funny Hats

Can you imagine a spectacular scene off the top of your head? How about turning it into an amazing party hat? You and your friends can make a game out of creating funny animals and characters, then assembling them into original hats you'll be proud to wear!

You can attach a piece of elastic to your hat. Pull it under your chin to help keep your hat on your head.

1
Draw your figures on the paper.

2
Cut them out, leaving a small tab at the bottom of each figure.

3
Paint your figures in bright colors and let them dry.

4
Find a small box that will easily stay on your head. Paint it and let dry.

5
Bend the tabs on your figures. Glue them to the top of your hat so they stand up.

6
You can add extra figures by gluing them to the ones that are already there. But be careful—don't overload your scene or it might collapse!

Coarse Salt Painting

Creative and fun, coarse salt painting is a technique that adds texture to your pictures and brilliance to your paint. It's a secret recipe that's sure to amaze your friends!

MATERIALS

- Black marker
- Corrugated cardboard
- Coarse salt
- Poster paint
- Paintbrushes

1 Using our models as inspiration, draw your picture on a square of corrugated cardboard.

2 In a bowl, mix a few pinches of coarse salt with poster paint.

3 Apply your paint mixture, leaving it in a thick layer. Don't spread it too thin.

4 Finish off with the details. As the paint dries, you'll notice the texture and brilliance it gives to your work of art.

145

Exotic Birds

Make an exotic flock of birds with interchangeable parts. Design some wild and wonderful wings, crazy crests, and fancy feet. Then have fun putting them together in unusual ways!

MATERIALS
- Grease pencil
- Tracing paper
- Corrugated cardboard
- Scissors
- Poster paint
- Paintbrushes

Use a grease pencil to draw the various bird parts on tracing paper. Turn the tracing paper over. Rub over the tracing paper to transfer the parts onto cardboard.

Cut out the pieces. Be sure to cut small notches in them so they'll fit together.

3 Paint all the pieces white. This white base will help you paint brighter colors later. Let dry.

4 Paint both sides of the pieces in a variety of colors. Let dry.

5 Decorate the painted pieces with dots, dashes, and other small patterns to give your birds an interesting variety of plumage.

6 Once dry, put your birds together in different combinations of crests, bodies, beaks, and feet.

Animal Mailboxes

You've got mail! With some paint and paper cutouts, you can turn a boring shoe box into a mailbox stamped with creativity!

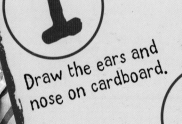

1 Draw the ears and nose on cardboard.

2 Cut them out carefully.

3 Paint the shoebox, ears, and nose black.

MATERIALS

- Shoe box
- Cardboard from another box
- Pencil or pen
- Scissors
- Colored paper
- Black paint
- Paintbrush
- Art knife
- Glue

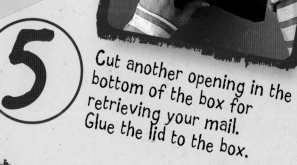

4 Use the art knife to cut a slit in one end of the shoebox so letters can be dropped in.

5 Cut another opening in the bottom of the box for retrieving your mail. Glue the lid to the box.

6 Tear strips and circles out of colored paper.

7 Decorate the box with the torn pieces of paper. Glue on the ears and any other face parts.

Wild Ostriches

MATERIALS
- Art knife
- Corks
- Glue
- Toothpicks
- Paint
- Paintbrushes
- Feathers or yarn
- Googly eyes

1 Using an art knife, cut two thin circles from the end of a cork. Use a cork for the head, another one for the body, and the two circles for the feet.

2 Next, using a little glue, assemble the corks and toothpicks as shown.

3 Paint a small cork for the beak. Then paint your ostrich and let dry.

4 Glue on the beak, feathers, and googly eyes.

Paper Bag Faces

Adding a splash of color and a few accessories can give a whole new life to old paper bags. You'll be amazed at how fast you can turn those sad sacks into smiling faces!

1 Draw the spots, eyes, ears, muzzle, tongue, and tail on white paper.

2 Paint the cow's spots and tail black. Paint the muzzle and tongue pink. Outline the eyes and ears in thick black marker.

MATERIALS
- Heavy white paper
- Black marker
- Scissors
- Paint
- Paintbrushes
- Paper bag
- Glue
- Shoelaces

3 Cut out all the pieces.

4 Fold the bottom part of the bag to make a flap. Slit the flap's end if you like. This will make the cow's face.

5 Glue the pieces on the bag, starting with the spots. Add shoelace pieces to the end of the cow's tail.

153

Cartoon Invitations

Invite your friends to your birthday party with these clever, unique cards. Start with cardboard, add cartoon characters, and don't forget a funny message!

It's my Birthday !!!

1 Cut a 4x6-inch rectangle out of cardboard. Draw a border along the edge, and add some musical notes to the background.

2 On another piece of cardboard, draw your animals or characters as well as a cartoon speech bubble. Cut them out.

3 Glue your characters onto the cardboard rectangle. Glue the speech bubble and write your message in it.

Jungle Mobiles

You'll get jungle fever after making this easy mobile. An old toothbrush comes in handy for creating the texture!

1

Draw six jungle animals on cardboard. Make them the same size, but give each one its own unique style.

2

Cut out the animals.

3

Paint them all the same color, using the toothbrush to splatter the paint, which will give them a spotted look. Let dry.

4

Make a small hole in the back and belly of each animal with the scissors. Pass nylon thread through the holes.

5

Hang three animals on the same length of thread, one above the other. Hang the other three in the same way on a separate thread.

6

Cut a 2-foot piece of metal wire and curl up the ends. Tie a set of hanging animals at each end.

Paperweight Fish

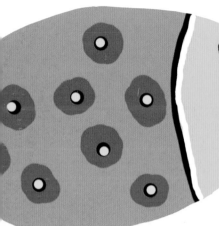

These plaster fish look like the smooth stones you find in rivers or on beaches. They make nice paperweights to give as gifts.

1 Follow the instructions for making the plaster. Mix it in the plastic container.

2 Coat the spoon with a little oil. Fill the spoon with plaster and hold it level.

If you happen to find some smooth stones when walking on the beach or in woods, you could paint these to use as paperweights, too!

3 Let the plaster harden, remove it from the spoon, and let it dry well.

Your fish will look best if you use bright colors and vivid designs. Remember to protect the table with newspapers and wear an apron as you work.

4 Draw your fish design on the plaster.

5 Paint the background colors first. Let the paint dry. Use a fine paintbrush for the little details.

Tube Fish

✂ MATERIALS
- Black marker
- Foam sheets in assorted colors
- Scissors
- Empty cosmetic tubes
- Stapler
- Modeling clay
- Wire
- Glue
- Acrylic paint
- Paintbrushes

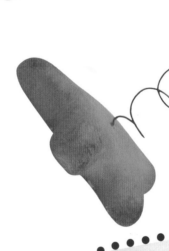

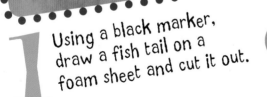
1 Using a black marker, draw a fish tail on a foam sheet and cut it out.

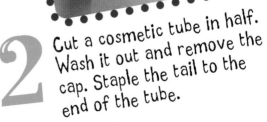
2 Cut a cosmetic tube in half. Wash it out and remove the cap. Staple the tail to the end of the tube.

3 Make a starfish out of modeling clay for the base. Curl the wire and insert it into the fish and the starfish.

4 Make eyes out of modeling clay, and glue them on. Paint the fish and the starfish.

Flying Saucer

With a yogurt cup, a soda bottle, and some paper plates, you can make a flying saucer that's out of this world. Or let your imagination run wild by using other recycled objects!

1
Cut the soda bottle 4 inches above the base. Attach the base to the back of a paper plate with tape. Glue the yogurt container, upside down, to the back of the second plate.

2
Wrap the yogurt container in crushed paper and secure it with tape.

3
Glue the two plates together edge to edge to make the flying saucer.

4
Paint your flying saucer, and add a few details like portholes and headlights. Attach a couple of toothpicks with cotton balls stuck on the ends to make the antennae.